Letters to my Children
In Retrospect a Surrender to Spirit

by

Johnnie James

Bloomington, IN  Milton Keynes, UK

authorHOUSE®

AuthorHouse™
1663 Liberty Drive, Suite 200
Bloomington, IN 47403
www.authorhouse.com
Phone: 1-800-839-8640

AuthorHouse™ UK Ltd.
500 Avebury Boulevard
Central Milton Keynes, MK9 2BE
www.authorhouse.co.uk
Phone: 08001974150

First published by AuthorHouse 3/1/2007

ISBN: 978-1-4259-6763-5 (sc)

Library of Congress Control Number: 2006909489

*Printed in the United States of America
Bloomington, Indiana*

This book is printed on acid-free paper.

"Life is lived forward but understood backward."

Soren Kierkegaard

INTRODUCTION

I often have thoughts running through my mind when I awaken in the from a somewhat sound sleep.

Recently, I've been waking consistently around 3:00 am unable to return to sleep, and on this morning, Spirit had a gift for me. These letters.

I'd always wanted to write a book, I write poetry, short stories, snippets, which more often than not end up in a file, waiting for an assignment.

There was something very different this time about the writing I was doing, I wasn't struggling with it. It simply flowed.

Everything was coming directly from my life experiences in a most unusual way. A series of letters to my children. I felt divinely inspired.

Coming from a background of major dysfunction, lack of integrity, lack of love, no boundaries. I was emotionally, physically, and sexually, abused, the abuse occurred throughout my young life in my family and in some instances extended family.

What is new about this sort of an experience is nothing, many people have experienced trauma in varying degrees, some talk about it, others act it out with destructive behavior.

I was evaluating my life and the lives of my children, and I felt somehow disappointed. As a parent I'd always wanted so much good for them, however, I lacked the consciousness necessary to prepare me for raising children, and providing them with the tools necessary for them to have all that I did not.

I wanted happiness, joy and success for my children that all rested in spiritual and holy choices, many of which I did not make.

Coming from such a background, living my life in shame, remorse and guilt, was equally as unhealthy as the suffering I endured while growing up. What does one do?

What I have learned through this process is that, this book is a healing a delving into the mysteries of Spirit and all the wonderful messages of life I may have missed for one reason or another, along my journey.

The wonderful part in all of this is I've been able to develop a relationship with Spirit that is absolutely divine. Through all the trials, tribulations and challanges, have come clarity, truth, hope, love, and peace of mind.

If I'd known all that I know now, I would never have had the relationship to spirit that I presently own. The "dark nights of the soul" eleveated my desire to become more conscious, consequently, I have much more to share.

I don't believe it is necessary to suffer to come to know Spirit, and I by no means recommend a life of despair or suffering to anyone. I was born into my despair and had to adapt to life as best I could. Eventually, the suffering that I experienced was so distressful and debilitating that I needed to end it. Deep within I'd always known there was a better way to live, I had only to choose life over death.

So although, the title says In Retrospect, it truly is a present work of awareness in direct relationship to the life I've experienced, and what has transpired from this life. I own all that I am and hope to become, all of which is significant, for my spiritual growth, and any and all who cross my path.

Never did I suspect that it would be a spiritual one, however; I'm very joyful and blessed to be writing these Letters to my Children. God Bless!

"The Lord works in mysterious ways his wonders to perform."
He perfecteth the thing which concerneth me.

To Grasshopper, Sister, & Lil M
Bam & Boogie
With Love and Gods Blessings

LETTER AT DAWN

～

"Man that is born of a woman is of few days, and full of trouble.
He cometh forth like a flower, and is cut down: he fleeth also as a shadow,
and continueth not". Job 14: 1-2

My dear ones it saddens me what I see as I look around, and evaluate our lives, and where we are. It <u>appears</u> as though it could be too late for us, but deep within I believe it is the dawning after all.

This is not a judgment, but an acceptance of choices made at a lesser consciousness a lack of awareness, which I wish for now, that I did not realize before.

Glancing back over our lives, I see clearly, often where I lacked awareness, made poor choices. I see with total clarity if I'd not done this then that would not have happened.

Interestingly enough, many times, most times I knew deep within that I was making poor decisions, but was in such an emotional state, that I did not care, giving no thought to what lie before me at the time.

This is not a bearing down on the past, or a hanging on to what was but a realization, of how "lack of consciousness" will deter one's life.

Ignorance is often the culprit in our lives, being mislead and lacking the proper tools for living a wholesome life. However; just living the Ten commandments could save anyone from much distress, if they were taught them and emulated them.

Example is also a great tool for living well, if one is blessed with proper guidance, one can learn how to live, how to best treat one another. People more often than not take their lessons from what life has shown them, from personal experience.

Being raised in a lie, a home filled with confusion and mixed messages and an almost non-existent value system, or lack of consciousness what one walks away with is best a fear based hopelessness of what life has to offer.

It's quite interesting, because in spite of my circumstance I had endless hope, and boundless desire to give you all that I never had, to make certain that your lives would not be my life. How was I to accomplish this?

"For the thing which I greatly feared is come upon me, and that which I was afraid of is come unto me." Job 3: 25

I did not know, I only knew that my heart was brimming with love for you and if I could demonstrate a life of peace, hope love, and success, all would be well. My love was not enough, life would be disappointing, we would each suffer tremendously, I would wonder why?

It would not be until much later, many trials behind me, much further along the journey that it all begin to make sense to come together in such a way that I would become aware, and begin to understand, that all that had happened was my path.

You as my children were integral to my experience. My wanting to live a life of value, give you such a life was all based on my consciousness.

Personally I believe we have each become pretty incredible individuals. Kind, generous, loving, and aware of the Spirit of God.

Love,
Mama

January 19, 2006

Dear Children,

I am taking solace in the fact that Divine Order is taking place in our lives, no matter the appearance. Although things appear to be falling apart, there is order in all things, and one element builds on the other and there is always a new order coming.

The key to the new order is what I am thinking, doing and being, these elements determine the new order and how it will develop. I am in dominion, I am conscious of what I am thinking, doing, being. I am.

Love,
Mama

Dear Lil'M,

I so wish I could have protected you from many of the experiences you were exposed to as a child, however; all our experiences have everything to do with who we become and why.

Without our experiences, even the awful ones we cannot grow, we would not stretch and move beyond. Our life experiences are our personal pilgrimage.

When I visited you abroad a few years back you mentioned a blaming discussion you and your friends were having a discussion which you held your parents responsible for all your life troubles and pain.

You shared with me in the midst of this discussion, a realization you had that your parents were not responsible for all your trials and the life you are living. Is your path, your destiny. Thank you.

Love,
Mama

January 19, 2006

Dear Sister,

Judge not that ye be not judged. For which what judgment ye judge, ye shall be judged; and with what measure ye mete, it shall be measured to you again. Matthew 7:1,2.

We must guard our thoughts, for our thoughts determine our experience. We believe what we do, the visible action demonstrated covers our judgments; however our thoughts count far more towards responses to us in life than, what we do, for our thoughts create our action.

Reflected to us is ourselves. The beauty we see in others or lack thereof, is always a reflection of ourselves. That is the role thoughts play our thoughts govern action. This is the Universal Law.

This idea is often difficult to grasp, because the things hidden deeply in our hearts, always reveal themselves in our lives, and unless we understand the principle of the law, we won't understand why.

Love,
Mom

January 19, 2006

Dear Grasshopper,

I was thinking about the road 237 returning home after that awful assault you witnessed that night. I apologize and wish I'd been more present, but honestly I was just as frightened as you.

What I have come to realize is that you were brought up in a spirit of fear.

"Thou therefore my son be strong in the grace that is in Christ Jesus"
2 Timothy 1

I fully understand why; but what you must realize is that fear is a crippling, oppressive emotion, and it can and will destroy us if we don't place our faith and trust in the spirit of God.

"Be not afraid of sudden fear, neither of the desolation of the wicked when it cometh" Proverbs 3:25

I was afraid too, and because of my fear, the worst came upon us.

Afraid of being alone, fear of having no family that cared for me, fear that I couldn't make a life for us, all because I did not believe enough to trust God's faithfulness towards me, towards us.

My faith was weak, my spirit was weak, my consciousness was that of a victim.

Love,
Mama

"Though I speak with the tongues of men and of angels, and have not charity, I am become as sounding brass, or a tinkling cymbal."
1 Corinthians 13:1

Dear children;

The spirit says I should speak of love today. I kept hearing these words in my mind, tinkling cymbal.

Love has been on my mind, and what love actually is, what love looks like. I've been combing the scriptures and the one verse above resounds very loudly to me.

Although we most often think of love as an emotion, a feeling, in actuality love is a demonstration and action. Our feelings do play a role in how we demonstrate love, however the feeling is not the love.

One must guard their heart to remain in loving action.

Our thinking again determines our outcome. Our thoughts create feelings, which in turn, create our heart. What we think, what we believe will develop in us feelings that create an attitude of love.

For my thoughts are not your thoughts, neither are your ways my ways, saith the Lord.

For as the heavens are higher that the earth, so are my ways higher than your ways, and my thoughts your thoughts. Isaiah 55: 8-9

*I've always **thought** of myself as a loving person, although I realize that in every case I have not been so.*

You my children, I have always loved. Although lately my thoughts have been challenged, due to disappointing behavior and attitudes I've been faced with, I've had to

9

reexamine my mindset to determine why I'm thinking as I am, what has caused my perspective to alter, causing my feelings to change.

Love,
Mama

If a man say, I love God, and hateth his brother, he is a liar: for he that loveth not his brother whom he hath seen, how can he Love God whom he hath not seen. I John 4:20

Many times our thoughts will change due to circumstances in our lives that cause us to feel differently about ourselves, others and our life circumstances. Thus the reason for guarding our hearts. To guard our hearts does not mean to hate, but to be cognizant of what we are carrying, feeling within.

Love governs everything, and although this is what I taught you, it is not what you witnessed, or experienced most of the time in your lives.

My poor choices, imposed on each of you; created experiences in your lives I sincerely did not desire you to have. Unfortunately my consciousness, was of such a state that I chose what was more despairing than blissful. My lack of faith, or putting aside of it created much havoc and despair for us all.

As far as love goes, if we would follow the first commandment and "Love our neighbors as ourselves", we would alleviate much despair.

Placing ourselves in others shoes, would create compassionate hearts, releasing judgments and increasing care one for the other, by better understanding another's plight, which would decrease the likelihood of our hearts becoming hard. It would make it easier to love, because in the other's shoes we can visualize their pain.

This follows the golden rule in the bible, "Therefore all things whatsoever ye would that men should do to you, do ye even so to them; for this is the law of the prophets." Matthew 7:12

Most times we don't take the time to consider another's plight and what living their experience may be like.

"And to godliness brotherly kindness; and to brotherly kindness charity." 2nd Peter 7.

Also in Hebrews 12:1-2, 9 find "Let brotherly love continue. be not forgetful to entertain strangers: for thereby some have entertained angels unawares."

Everything I am sharing with you is a demonstration of my love for each of you, you are lovely individuals, handmade by God; who deserve to have the best life. You have suffered immensely, and although you are very intelligent people and much of what I am sharing you know and understand; I felt compelled to write these letters to you.

Love,
Mama

CONTEMPLATION:

It makes no sense at all to do anything but worship God.

When I speak of God, I mean the spirit that God is, the Omnipresence, Omnipotent, Omniscience spirit.

I've lived a full life having accomplished many things some of which I am not proud. Errs that have caused me great sadness and shame. I have also lived my life consciously strictly adhering to Gods will and finding purpose for my life. At these times I have found more joy than ever, in righteousness there is peace.

There is nothing better than being in communion with God. My life is so much fuller, joyful, blessed and whole when I walk with God. Even during times of difficulty, when I often don't know what the outcome will be it is always more fulfilling.

I have fewer questions, I wonder less about outcome and have more wonderment about life, because I know the will of God is always for my best. Regardless of the appearance or circumstance surrounding the situation.

I know that each experience that has occurred in my life, goes to glorify and show forth the greatness of the awesome Spirit of God, thus I no longer have questions, I live to do God's will. I Let Go, I Let God!

But Jesus said, "Suffer little children, and forbid them not, to come Unto me for of such is the kingdom of heaven."

Dear Children;

"Even a child is known by his doings, whether it be pure and whether it be right." Proverbs 10:11

Growing up as you did, your lives were should I say challenging to say the least. Challenging due to the fact that life is a challenge.

As a parent my responsibility was to guide you in the proper way, the ways of GOD, (spirit) so that you would have proper tools to live by.

With these tools, regardless the circumstances or situations you found yourselves in, you would know in your heart of hearts that all was not lost, whatever was placed before you to endure.

Your heart must first have been made strong, in the word, and your understanding of it, so that you were prepared when the trials came. You would know where to turn in times of distress and trouble. In life if the foundation is never built, there is no stability so one gets tossed about with no real sense of self no proper orientation due to lack of example.

"He is like a man which built a house and digged deep, and laid the foundation on a rock and when the flood came, the stream beat vehemently upon the house, and could not shake it."
"But he that heareth and doeth not, is like a man that without a foundation built a house upon the earth; against which the stream did beat vehemently, and immediately it fell." Luke 6:48-49

Parents are responsible for their children, to lead and guide them, to show them their way, as stated in Proverbs 22:6

"Train up a child in the way he should go: and when he is old, he will not depart from it."

If this does not occur the result is a host of maladies which create confusion, fear, distress, resentment, hatred and a whole host of things that one must resolve.

Situations such as this make life so much more challenging, and causes great difficulty, although even to the good and best some rain does come.

"That ye may be the Sons of your Father which is in heaven: He causes the sun to rise on the just and the unjust, and sends rain on the righteous and unrighteous." Matthew 5:45

I have done this to you, however; my ignorance, lack of consciousness, and disregard for the word placed each of you in regrettable situations, none of which I can change now.

What I can do is share with you the better route of life and the best way one should live no matter what the challenges that came before. by putting one's faith and trust in God, living a spiritual life focusing on what is honorable and good, is the only success.

Coming from a life fraught with troubles, pain, deceit, abuse and sadness, I had to learn to live a life of love, respect, honor, interity and decency, a spiritual life.

My life has always been a work in progress. I'm still not where I'd like to be, I am still learning.

We somehow select the place we're in based on our consciousness or lack of it, what we experience and where we find ourselves is where we should be in order to approximate our life purpose. God knows every hair on our head, knows everything about us, sees our hearts,there is nothing we do that Spirit lacks awareness of.

Jesus Christ came into the world as God on earth to die for our sins, how much more clear can it be. That was the purpose for his life. If Christ had a purpose why wouldn't we?

All our challenges, sufferings, difficulties, our pain has purpose, And we must strive to discover what that purpose is!

To the degree that we learn who we are, and why we're here no matter what occurs in our lives, we are fulfilling our purpose and coming closer to who we truly are and what our gift to the world is.

The more conscious we become, the more clarity we gain, the more we grow, the more knowledge we gain. We're here by divine appointment,God is perfect we're part of that perfection.

I Love you,
Mama

"Honor thy father and thy mother that thy days may be long upon the earth, which the Lord thy God has given thee."

"Train up a child in the way he should go and when he is old he will not depart from it."

"Suffer the little children to come unto me for of such is the kingdom of God."

Dear Children:

Parents purpose is to teach, provide your material needs and give spiritual guidance to you.

Consequently, God has a twofold agenda here. As parents our responsibility is to teach and train our children in the spiritual ways, and our children are to honor us as parents.

Parents have the responsibility to govern their children spiritually, and children have the responsibility to honor those parents for doing so.

As parents we must do all that we can to arouse spiritual curiosity in our children, teaching them all we know about GOD, and what it means to lead a spiritual life, which imparts incredible benefits for them and their lives. Creating for them a platform a springboard to enter into the arena of life.

Life is difficult, however; with the proper tools, the difficulties can be diminished tremendously, if our children who they are, their relationship to Spirit. It is our responsibility of parents, to reveal these truths to our children by word and deed.

Children in turn, should be grateful for the work we as parents do in preparation of assisting them in moving forward towards their optimum achievements in life through us by God's grace.

Unfortunately, our lives don't always work out in this way. Some parents come from miserable backgrounds, as did their parents. There was no spiritual foundation, children grew up being horribly mistreated, and abused.

Mixed messages are sent, there is lack of proper guidance, some are left to their own devices, raising themselves. There are numerous scenarios more than I can mention. And personally children, I've come to believe anything that moves a child away from God is abuse, because the only life is the life of spirit, any other life is without value.

Then what? When our earthly parents fail in their duties towards their children, God's grace and mercy will sustain them throughout their experience leading them towards their good in life.

Divine guidance, and order, the invisible realm does the work as spirit which is infinite in power. God's Omnipotence, _can_ bring bountiful mercy and grace upon our lovely little children and bring them through any sort of experience that does not resonate for good.

God is love. Whomever lives in love lives in God, and God in them. There is no fear in love. Perfect love drives out fear, because fear has to do with punishment. The one who fears is not made perfect in love.

God looks into our hearts, and knows our desires, even as little children and having a heart for God is a blessing, and we will never be forsaken if our hearts are so.

Love,
Mama

Do not seek revenge or bear a grudge against one of you people, but love your neighbor as yourself: I am the Lord." Leviticus 19:18

Vengeance is mine, I shalt repay says the Lord of Hosts

Dear Children:

Grudges and vengeance emerge from a bitter root. Unfortunately bitterness emerges from an inability to forgive, a looking outward.

This is not to say that the pain you may have is not real, however; as truly spiritual beings we must develop the capacity to forgive, releasing those who have hurt us, in order to fulfill our own destinies.

Truth is you've been hurt, your life is not what you believe it should be, you've suffered based on the ignorance and mistakes of others and it is painful. Remember, whomever has hurt you has gotten away with nothing, They must revisit what they have done. More the reason to forgive.

No matter, forgiveness must be your priority; holding grudges, and wishing to take revenge on others for the pain they've caused, only creates more pain. It is self destructive!

Holding hurts in your heart you have experienced, not allowing yourself to move beyond only causes more pain and perpetuates the problem. Although many injustices have been brought to bear against you, it is your responsibility to yourself to move forward in a spirit of love.

In forgiveness we can create a new paradigm, begin to heal and end the cycle of injustice. Your forgiveness of others heals you, you forgive for you!

Love,
Mama

"God is Love. Whoever lives in love lives in God and God in him."
John 19:16

Dear Children:

In all matters of life, everything is love. Love is absolutely the only thing there is. There is only one power, which is the power and Spirit of God God is Love!

Consequently, if we can love enough, all things can be healed. Love creates an incredible life. A life of value.

Lack of love,and compassion for others is why there exists so much pain in our society, nation and the world. Every problem exists, because people don't know how to love.

We are made in the image, we are the substance and essence of God; we are Love.

Love,
Mama

CONTEMPLATION:

God is absolutely awesome. Isn't it wonderful when from all appearances, things seem to be falling down all around you but you know deep within that all is well.

Nothing appears to be working. What you see visibly, in no way reveals the power of God.

But then God shows up, not to say he was ever away, because of course that is not the case.

Circumstances clear up in a great way, things that have fallen apart come together. God shows up! God's amazing grace and power takes the reins and moves mountains. God shows up. Yes!

God is Faith!

Dear Children:

Love is gentle, love is integrity, respect, honor, compassion.

Love is peaceful, and harmonious, joy filled, joyful all that is good.

You know you're in love when you're feeling and acting in these ways.

Any feelings outside of these is love amiss. Someone has lost their way, and live outside the reality of love; instead they express, resentment, hostility, fear, hatred, envy, jealousy, anger, shame and unforgiveness.

These feelings cause them to behave in ways that are not conducive to A spiritual path and the ways of God of good.

It's actually quite simple in theory, if you know this, live this, You're in your true essence. Try being love.

Love,
Mama

"So if anyone is in Christ, there is a new creation: everything old has passed away; see, everything has become new!" 2 Corinthians 5:17

Dear Children:

Choices, inspired by reality, reality inspired by love or fear; determines the outcome. If there is no intervention, along the way the loving behavior will only grow and enhance the life of the individual who embraces it and they will grow in the way of God.

The opposite being choices inspired by fear, will do the same, the individual inspired by a reality of fear will be fearful and live their lives as such enhancing their fears and growing away from the good of God.

Chances are there will be intervention in both situations, and love will see fear and fear will see love, and whether or not the other will take over is the question. What choices will be made in life to either enhance their good, or increase their vice. Which?

The choices that were made for you were of course not your own, but once you have gained knowledge of your own accord, and you have the Divine guidance and intelligence to determine your direction, you can create the reality you wish.

You must create the life you desire you are free to decide; by searching, for the face of God which you are the essence of, are created in the image of your being the substance of.

You must choose, and will be responsible for your choices, no matter what came before! I wonder if God lives in the past? I think not.

Love,
Mama

Moments

Our lives successive moments, lending one to the other.
Moments in time, building units of another,
Elation to moments of sadness,
Moments of grief to gladness
Moments of weakness and others of strength
Times of loss to gain and increase.
Fleeting moments in time of change to same;
Ephemeral moments, never to remain,
Increments of time, moments of change do not remain.

Moments clearly seen and sometimes muddled be
Time filled with loneliness, other moments accompaniment
Moments laden with riches divine, while lack ushers in moments more.

From moments of fear to moments of valor,
Loving moments to hatred unfolding
Angst to moments of jest
Moments of knowing, evolve to growing,
Rapid increments of time, our lives are only.
Moment by moment or temporal knowing.

Seasons from moments do come
Times we long to swiftly move beyond
Memories we wish to stay, but quickly only fade away.
Other moments become
Past, Present, Future life goes on.

Choices, decisions, circumstances abound.
By moments in time accompanied by,
Moments of grace, moments of mercy,
Wisdom filled moments to assist us to glory.

Moment to moment our lives we've created.
Do take heart in the moment, the power in it
Create glorious splendor, or sinister visions
What may be our choices, momentarily we create,
momentarily we make.

Our life full of tiny moments, of great magnitude
Moment by moment our only knowing
Moment by moment our lives are growing!

January 28, 2006

"To everything there is a season, and a time to every purpose under the heaven." Ecclesiastes 3:1

Dear Children:

Timing came to me today. Everything is cyclical, we live our lives in cycles. Everything that occurs based on our choices is mean't to be, there are no coincidences, no mistakes.

To live is to ebb and flow like the tides of the seas; passing from high points to low, and at other times to flow or, abound with smooth uninterrupted movement; or to at other times, to be catapulted forward like the power of a waterfall, the rushing vortex of the cascading waters down from its point of power leaving one with no real control of the situation or firmly catapulting one forward to still waters. Such is life.

When we understand the state that we are in, and when we cast our burdens on the Christ within, it becomes much easier to accept our situation, and move beyond.

What happens when we try and fight against what is, using our own will, we create a whirlwind, a personal state of confusion that continues until we get it. Just be!

Love,
Mama

CONTEMPLATION:

I know what I know because of my relationship with God, and even more importantly because I lack perfection and have through more awareness (consciousness) come to know who I am.

If I had always done the thing that is right, or acceptable or more plausible, based on society's mores I would not know anything, because all that I did would be based on the approval of others, and in my urgency to please (which I have done) I would not recognize myself remotely.

I would live by the temporal rules of this society, their caste system, only to still suffer the slights that one suffers by not fitting the bill, in one way or the other. Not having, not knowing, not being connected, the list goes on and on.

To retreat from this, and to examine for ones self what life is about, realizing that it isn't based on others, their thoughts, their approvals, their ways, but is personal in every sense of the word, and to create an identity that is realistic and spiritual is the only true life. The only way.

In the spiritual sense, there is no division, we are all connected, we are all the same, cut from the same cloth, we are all branches, leaves or fruit on the tree of life. We are all nourished and created from the same source, the same essence, the same substance.

The tree of life!

"You got a right, I gota right.
We all got a right to the tree of life.

The very time I thought I was lost,
The dungeon shook and the chain fell off."

James Weldon and
J. Rosamond Johnson

"Wisdom is the principal thing; therefore get wisdom: and with all the getting get understanding." Proverbs 4:7

"It is the human beings inner head which brings relief, say the knowledge holders. The human being should consult first the inner-head, say the knowledge holders. The inner head will lead the human being to the proper source."

Dear Children:

Awareness, Consciousness are one in the same. To have a mind that is any one of these is possessing wisdom in and of itself.

To lack these qualities is to live in ignorance, disconnected from reality of Spirit, in a state of utter despair, spiritual destitution and quiet desperation.

One must know the heart and mind of Spirit, and in knowing one's own heart and mind, therein does their answer lie.

When I embrace God, I embrace myself!

Love,
Mama

CONTEMPLATION:

I've been contemplating prayer, change, and desire the connection between them. I realized there really should be none.

I've decided that I will never request Spirit to change anything again.

I won't try to get a quick fix, or place a special request to modify my life circumstances.

I'll wait expectantly for the outcome. I'll have full faith in the process, and trust God vehemently. My reason for coming to this is I've finally realized that everything in our lives is divinely ordered. there just are no accidents, there are no mistakes, not when it comes to Spirit.

All is exactly as it should be at each moment in time, to pray for an alteration or an adjustment is to meddle. I will be grateful for all things, be they to my liking or not.

"Existence has a face on every side and every face teaches a lesson. those who fully understand existence do not separate the faces from the lessons; Every lesson reveals aspects of Cosmic Law."

If I'm in the valley, I'm not going to ask for a fast pass to the peak. I'm in the valley for a reason,there is something in it I must experience, to pass go, with a bonus isn't going to give me the necessary awareness I need. No shortcuts, I'll only end up in the same valley again.

I need to methodically, and purposefully take the trek from valley to peak in order to resolve my issues and fulfill my highest good, and to cognize the divinely ordained appointment God has for me. Feel my fear!

If God knows, every hair on my head, then God knows where I need to be, and what I need to be doing at any given moment. Its my divine appointment.

To pray for release from something, or to request something that I may not deserve or be spiritually prepared for is to work against my own good.

God's faithfulness, abundant mercy and grace is far more than I could ever be worthy of, and the nerve of me to request spirit to do anything!

Dear Mama and Daddy;

I awakened this morning, feeling some anguish, about my life.

Although I realize that I am truly blessed, I was feeling more human than spirit, and feeling fear.

I was thinking of an event that I would attend next month, actually on my birthday, and it is to do with women in unfortunate circumstances, abused, beaten.

Gradually my thoughts went to my daughter, who I am estranged from, and I was wondering if she might be there, and what that would feel like to meet her under those circumstances.

Then Mama, I thought about you, and how much I'd like to call and speak with you, see how you're doing.

I know that I am tremendously blessed, however; there are times in life when you wish for things to be different. I'd just been contemplating The day prior, how I'd not request spirit to change a thing in my life, I'd accept all circumstances, as divinely ordered and appointed to and for my good.

I prayed to that effect, only claiming that I obtain more Divine intelligence, and wisdom as I make my way through. This knowledge would assist me in getting through what I consider my trials, or my valley.

I said to God, how grateful I was to have just an ounce of the essence of such a spirit, and how awesome it is to be made of such substance, and what a wonderful father he has been to me, since daddy could not.

I thought I should write you two, because it occurred to me that maybe deep in my heart of hearts I had not forgiven you, however this letter is to share with you that I accept all of my life, every part and parcel, and I know life was a bit overwhelming for the two of you, but you did your best, with the consciousness you possessed.

I'm grateful that in spite of everything, I had a heart of love, for God is love, and I always wanted to understand you and love you regardless.

I want to thank you for being who you were, and for being who you are, and most importantly I'd like you to know that I forgive and love you both dearly.

Love your,
daughter

February 1, 2006

CONTEMPLATION:

God is with me!

Dear Children:

Healing keeps appearing in my thoughts, and what came to mind, was a book written by Toni Cade Bambara, called the Salteaters. In this book was a young women named Velma, who was displeased with the circumstances of her life, and attempted suicide.

Well the community village that she lived in, was very involved in the lives of it's inhabitants, so a group of healers in the community got together to attempt to heal Velma, and before starting the process they asked.

"Just so's you're sure sweetheart, and ready to be healed, cause wholeness is no trifling matter. A lot of weight when you're well."

To be whole requires a personal commitment, it requires hope, faith and strength to move beyond what was to what is before you. Knowledge of the spirit within is required to know without doubt who and what you are. your value, your pedigree, your worth. You emerge from a long line of royalty, Kings, & Queens, and you must never underestimate your value, no matter what the circumstance you must always believe yourself worthy of all good.

You must remember you're a child of God substance of Spirit's substance, and when appearances don't support your path, know that to go within the answer will be found.

"There is no aligning without centering, messages cannot be sent without centering."

God has a purpose for everything, and when you understand the concepts of consciousness you realize that you have the personal power to create a healthier view of your life and the circumstances surrounding it.

You and you alone have the ability to see and sense beyond what is to what can be. Only you can heal yourself. You must want to be whole!

When you decide that where you are is no longer where you'd like to be, when you decide that nothing has to be quite as difficult as it is, and that you are the energy, the substance, the beauty and the awe of life, yes you. You will be made whole.

Love,
Mama

CONTEMPLATION:

I feel so in awe of God. I am forever amazed at each of the rare and wonderful qualities possessed by you.

I am so grateful to have a guide such as you. Such lasting faithfulness, grace and mercy, never ending do you lavish upon me.

I gaze in wonderment at all you have created and know there is absolutely none other than you. Your amazing faithfulness and consideration for me is always more than I can ask or accept, knowing myself as I do; however; you always choose to look beyond my infirmities and hold me in your everlasting arms of Grace, Strength, Mercy, power and above all your great abiding Love.

How fortunate I am to know of you and to have relationship with one so great. I never know what to say in description of you, I become tongue tied, searching for words in my limited vocabulary that aptly describe what I feel in my heart.

I am overwhelmed of sounding phony because I so want to describe your magnificence and your significance to me.

I am almost ashamed of not being able to express more succinctly who you are to me! What is in my heart.

In awe of you
Your love so true
A rarity
It is to me

When I gaze at and see around
The way of the world
I see no gift so rare
Your love to me

A faithful chalice
A friend forever
No judgment ever
My way doth come

A gentle feeling
I always feel
A heavy load of love
I carry
Will not allow
Hatred to tarry
In my soul

A pleasant memory
I constantly carry
To know you
Always with me be
Endearing to me your gracious spirit
Your love so true

A love unchanging
No questions enter
Unto me
That I change
Just be

Learning of you
Enlightens my path
Steps further taken
No more astray
So gently guided
Led to the light
There is no struggle
No pain, nor strife

A love unchanging
No questions enter
Unto me
Should I change
But only
Just be

Me

Dear Children:

Evil and the devil are considered major forces in our world. The Duality concept. Many people cannot live without these beliefs.

We have been indoctrinated with the belief of an evil creature from below roaming about the earth manifesting all sorts of wrongdoing and crisis through us, because of us and to us.

God created each of us in his image. It is clearly stated: God saw all that he had made and it was very good. Genesis 1:31

We are made in God's image, God is love, God is good, so where does this incipient demon come from? Suddenly do we get evil not good, devil from all that is good.

How could a demon, something evil come from all that is love and all that is good? How?

Spiritually speaking our thoughts, create our reasoning, our consciousness creates our reality.

We are not taught we are essence and substance of the Spirit of God.

We don't grow into the belief of our goodness, instead we are taught to focus on our faults, our infirmities without which we would need a devil.

No devil, no evil, no duality.

Without the awareness necessary to rise above certain circumstances one can feel prey to a life of despair, therefore; getting a false start, lacking the necessary knowledge and motivation to move forward. It is easier to accept a duality concept because from all appearances there are two.

If for any reason our beginnings weren't wholesome and much of what was demonstrated to us was destructive then there is reason to question goodness. Perhaps we are constantly looking over our shoulders for some lurking evil that controls our destinies.

Feelings of fear, shame, despair, guilt, hopelessness, condemnation, apathy, grief these are your devil.

Thinking thoughts such as these will not produce joy, peace, hope, faith, love or compassion.

Look beyond faulty demonstrations full of confusion, dismiss and rebuke the thoughts that create doubt and anxiety within you, causing you to question your value, your ability and move forward in your Christ consciousness.

Choose love, joy, success and prosperity. We are thinking spirits, Our minds cognize and can create any reality we choose.

If we think on a gutter level we're doomed to have gutter experiences. If we don't desire to live a life of poverty, strife, pain and sorrow we must rethink our lives to be that which we do desire.

Harsh thoughts bring harsher results and experiences. We draw to ourselves who and what we are. We think love, and we will receive love.

It is so important to be aware of your thoughts, what you're thinking because it determines everything in your life. Not the devil, nor evil but if your mind is operating at a lower consciousness, a devil consciousness then what you'll get is that gutter experience and you must decide to change that! When you change your mind, your life changes.

Have you ever noticed periods when it seemed people were exceptionally kind to you, very loving towards you *for no apparent reason. When this happens, what you are witnessing is an emulation of your self.*

You created that action in the other person, which in turn created this incredible experience of good feelings to and for you. Your love, light and kindness was reflected back to you.

When you're experiencing dark moments, and your attitude vibrates that darkness, it's only the anger, hostility and resentment you express or vibrate that you receive in return. Think about it.

Always be aware of your thoughts, they determine everything in your life. Putting aside all despair, no matter the appearance is key.

The only evil, the only true devil, is not realizing the mind of Christ within you. Your beauty your goodness, your gentleness, your spiritual greatness.

Flip the evil and live!

What you most think on, is what appears in your life.

Love,
Mama

February 7, 2006

When your intention changes so does your course and what seem to be miraculous events show up to support your new direction!

CONTEMPLATION: It's divine intervention when you didn't plan it, When it's happening without your conscious knowledge of how you got there.

Everything I've written has been inspired by spirit. I remembered when I was talking with my daughter that I dreamed that I saw a book with my name on it, six or seven months ago. I pretty much dismissed it after

I told her, and went about my life.

The book is now being written. Be cognizant, everything counts, nothing is too trivial or inconsequential, nothing.

We are mental spirits, and when we are divinely inspired, it is a gift.

Simply because we didn't plan for something to happen, or because it may seem out of character even weird at times, beyond our knowing, don't discount anything. Be conscious and follow the promptings that come in your life. Experience, just be!

Oh, and never tell yourself you can't do something that you're doing!

Dear Children;

To be selfless is the finest attribute a person can have.

A Selfless spirit is an absolute blessing, and is everything to do with our prosperity.

To possess a heart of generosity is to have a heart of faith. There are numerous incidents in the bible that support this premise.

"Cast thy bread upon the waters", It is more blessed to give than to receive"

To him who hath much, much is required. I could go on and on regarding this subject.

Being selfless requires that you give up your ego self, you are less self involved. Selflessness is an acknowledgement of what your capacity is, and as large as your ability to give, that much larger is your opportunity to receive.

To believe you do not have, is not to have! An attitude such as this will always impede anything you would like to accomplish in life.

If you believe you haven't enough to share with others you will not, and thus be distracted out of the exchange of life; this is the absolute truth. You will hold tightly to what you have, not releasing and observing it diminish.

You will live according to your beliefs and you will continue to perpetuate lack in your life based on fear of the same. "As a man thinketh so is he" You will create exactly in your life what your are thinking. A belief in lack creates a reality of the same.

"If what is to be offered is not one's own, then how can it be a sacrifice, say the knowledge-holders? What is precious is given up for something more precious, say the knowledge-holders."

We've been blessed with all that we have. Our fear causes us to hold back, grasping tightly what we have, however; it is ours only to the degree that we give as has been given to us.

A smile, a hell-o, a thank you, giving a gift where needed, sharing what you have although, you may not believe you have much, to give of yourself, is the greatest gift of all.

A selfless individual can teach others the principal, by demonstration of the practice or principal of giving in their lives. It is the multiplication principle what Jesus demonstrated when he manifested more bread and fish to feed the pilgrimage of the multitudes who faithfully followed to hear his teachings.

We are all in reciprocity, and selflessness is the truest form of this that I know. Realize that the more you give, the more will be added unto you. Give with a heart of love, and the kingdom is yours!

Joy may be at your headboard, while sorrow awaits at your feet, For they embody one another.

Love You,
Mom

CONTEMPLATION:

We must not grasp to tightly our disappointments, we must not regret that we were happy before we were sad.

"Take away the miseries and you take away some folks'reason for living."

We must see the underlying good in everything, because it is always there.

Life's disappointments are lessons in character building, in creating strength in us, one of life's journeys that is consistently leading us to our final destination, only to depart on another journey again.

Learn from them and release them.   Forget the disappointments to the degree that you will not allow them to deter you from your purpose, from your joy, from your next journey.

To the renewing of your spirit your true purpose.

There would be nothing if there were not you.
No refuge, no solace, no restitude.
No place to go in times of sadness
No one to praise in times of gladness

Where would we go, what would we do
Without you!

Love would not exist
Peace we could not experience
Graciousness we would not know
Your mercy would not flow

There would be nothing if there were not you
No realization of what could be
Without the presence of you

If there were not you
What love would preside
What, how, could life reside
In depleted spirits
Lacking all that is of life

There would be nothing if there were not you
I often wonder what I would do?
Without your promise, without your care
What life would look like
If you presence were not here

Your fullness, your loving, you gentle
Your peace, a spirit of richness, without
Leaves deplete, a world full of angst,
Confusion and doubt, a hopeless rejection
Of what life is about

There would be nothing if there were not you
I often wonder what I would do, if there were not you!

Dear Children:

I was considering life, and how precious your lives were to me, when you were in my womb. I anticipated absolutely every possibility, when your were being formed, I mean everything, based on my limited or expansive knowledge, however one sees it.

I ate well, got plenty of rest, guarded the material I consumed, (to the degree that I understood that principle at that time). I exercised, walked mostly, and read, or should I say gobbled up all the information I could on having a child, what the newest technology was, whatever I could do to prepare for your coming is what I did.

I wanted you to have a great start, to show up with all the tools necessary to be capable to navigate in this society, this world.

I did not desire as much for you as myself that you would come or arrive with anything lacking, anything that would hinder your successes.

This was my part. There was much I did not know, and with each subsequent pregnancy I gained more knowledge, and did improve.

I can look at each of you and take notice of where I was psychologically when I was carrying you.

Who you are, your progress, your presence of mind, (mindset), all of this is very much an indication of me.

I most ardently knew to love you, and care for you and that is exactly what I did. God did the rest!

You are each here for a reason, please realize exactly how special you are and that whatever it is that you yearn for most, is what you're here to do, to give, to be, please just be it, do it, give it, because this your purpose.

    Love you & may God's Blessings always be yours,

Mom

The Beginning

⌒

God – Diety: The Supreme Being, the Absolute, Eternal Infinite, Spirit, Reality or Truth in its absolute sense.

Jesus – (as revelation of the will of God) The life and teaching of Jesus illustrate the nature of reality as love, wisdom and law. The Divine nature and Divine will are one.

Lord - Refers to the Universal "I Am" operating through the Individual I. <u>Conscious</u> use of this Spiritual power is our true Savior.

Christ Jesus - (mind) the that was in Christ Jesus The universal sense of goodness and unity upon which Jesus Based his thinking.

Love - The outpouring of Spirit. The givingness of Life. In its Lesser sense, the affection one has for another. The great Transforming power, which brings everything into harmony. Unifying Principle, the creative element, the motivation Power of all that is fine and noble in life.

Spirit – Life essence which permeates all persons and all things. The thing within everything which makes it what it is. God the Living Spirit Almighty.

Heaven – Harmony, Wholeness, Health, Physical Wellness, Happiness, Mental Peace, poise and well being.

Devil – Anything which denies the unity of good, the allness of truth, Or our oneness with Spirit.

Omnipotence-Omnipresence-Omniscience – Spirit is All Power, All Prescence and All Wisdom.

NOTES & QUOTES

1 *Peter Erskine African Openings to the Tree of Life. (Berkeley: Regent Press 1987). P.1, 11, 21 & 29*

2 *Ernest Holmes New Thought Dictionary. (DeVorss & Company 1991) .34,51,58,72,84,135*

3 *Holy Bible Quotations, King James Version, New International Version*

4 *Toni Cade Bambara The Salt Eaters (Vintage Books 1992) P.10,16*